LEVEL 2

BOOKKEEPING AND COSTING FLASHCARDS

BY TERESA CLARKE

LEVEL 2 BOOK OF FLASHCARDS FOR BOOKKEEPING AND COSTING

This book is full of ideas for you to create your own flashcards for your Level 2 studies. They are loosely divided between bookkeeping and costing flashcards, but some topics will overlap.

Contents

Part 1

BOOKKEEPING FLASHCARDS

DEAD CLIC

Debits increase
Expenses
Assets
Drawings

Credits increase
Liabilities
Income
Capital

THE ACCOUNTING EQUATION

Assets – Liabilities = Capital

DUAL EFFECT

Every debit entry must have a corresponding credit entry of the same value.

Example:

Dr	Office Expenses		£50
Cr	Bank	£50	

CAPITAL AND REVENUE EXPENDITURE

Capital expenditure is money spent on the purchase of assets or major improvements to them.

Revenue expenditure is money spent on day-to-day expenses for the running of the business.

ASSET OR LIABILITY

An asset is money or items that the business <u>owns</u> or something that is owed to it.

A liability is money that the business <u>owes</u> to others.

NON-CURRENT ASSET

An asset which the business is likely to own for more than one year, such as a vehicle, equipment, or factory premises.

NON-CURRENT LIABILITY

A liability which the business is likely to still owe for more than 12 months. This is usually a long term loan or mortgage of premises.

TRIAL BALANCE

A list of all the ledger balances into debit and credit columns. The two columns should equal the same amount.

PETTY CASH

A small amount of cash kept by the business for payment of small expenses.

Often kept in a petty cash tin.

CASH BOOK

A record of money received by the business and paid out by the business.

Sometimes split into the CASH RECEIPTS BOOK and CASH PAYMENTS BOOK.

INVOICE

A document sent to a customer by the business requesting payment for a product or service.

RECONCILIATION

A comparison of records to check for errors, such as a bank reconciliation or petty cash reconciliation.

DEPRECIATION

The amount by which a non-current asset goes down in value in each.

A car may cost £10,000, but by the end of the first year is worth £9,000. The depreciation expense in that year was £1,000.

CREDIT NOTE

A document sent to a customer by the business refunding money for goods returned.

Can be used against outstanding invoices for a credit customer.

SALES DAY BOOK

A record of sales invoices sent to customers.

SALES RETURNS DAY BOOK

A record of credit notes issued to customers for goods returned to the business.

PURCHASES DAY BOOK

A record of purchase invoices received from suppliers.

PURCHASE RETURNS DAY BOOK

A record of credit notes received from suppliers for goods returned by the business.

DISCOUNTS ALLOWED DAY BOOK

A record of discounts given to customers by the business.

DISCOUNTS RECEIVED DAY BOOK

A record of discounts given received by the business from suppliers.

REVENUE

Income from sales made or services provided by the business.

Alternative words:
Sales / Income / Sales Revenue / Sales Income

INVENTORY

Opening inventory is the stock held at the start of the year. Stock is goods for re-sale.

Closing inventory is the stock held at the end of the year.

TRADE RECEIVABLES

Money owed to the business by its customers.

Also known as the:

SALES LEDGER CONTROL ACCOUNT

Or

RECEIVABLES LEDGER CONTROL ACCOUNT.

TRADE PAYABLES

Money owed by the business to its suppliers.

Also known as the:

PURCHASES LEDGER CONTROL ACCOUNT

Or

PAYABLES LEDGER CONTROL ACCOUNT.

CAPITAL

Money invested into the business by the owner and owed back to the owner by the business.

This is a liability for the business because the business OWES the money to the owner.

DRAWINGS

Money or goods taken out of the business by the owner for their own use.

CALCULATING VAT

VAT Inclusive figure at 20% - including VAT

£240 / 120 x 100 = net amount
£240 / 120 x 20 = net amount

VAT Exclusive figure at 20% - excluding VAT

£200 x 20% = VAT
£200 + VAT = gross amount

Net + VAT = Gross

TRADE DISCOUNT

A trade discount is taken off before VAT is applied.

List price, less trade discount, then multiplied by the VAT rate.

BULK DISCOUNT

A discount given when a certain quantity is ordered in one go.

Bulk discount is taken off before VAT is applied.

List price, less bulk discount, then multiplied by the VAT rate.

SETTLEMENT DISCOUNT

A discount is given only when the customer pays by a certain date.

Also known as EARLY PAYMENT DISCOUNT.

The invoice is sent out at full amount and discount only calculated if the customer pays within a specified time. Then a credit note is issued for the discount given.

BUSINESS ENTITY

For accounting purposes, a business is a separate entity from the owner.

For a sole trader or partnership this means that the owners' personal assets and liabilities are kept separate from those of the business.

The expenses of the business are kept separate from the private expenses of the owner or owners.

DIRECT DEBIT

A direct debit is authorised by the business to take varying amounts each month from the business bank account, such as a telephone expense.

STANDING ORDER

A standing order is set up by the business to pay the same amount each month from the business bank account, such as rent.

LOAN

Money borrowed by the business from a bank or other organisation/individual.

This is a credit because it is money owed to others.

BAD DEBT / IRRECOVERABLE DEBT

Money owed to the business which is very unlikely to be paid.

Dr Irrecoverable Debt Expense
Cr Trade Receivables

CASTING ERROR

Casting means adding, so casting error is an "adding up" error.

CONTRA ENTRY / SET-OFF ENTRY

This occurs when a customer is also a supplier.

A customer owes the business £10. That customer is also a supplier of the business, and the business owes them £10. We cancel this out.

Dr Payables £10 (lowering the balance)
Cr Receivables £10 (lowering the balance)
BOTH accounts will always be reduced.

EXTRACTION ERROR

Extraction means removal (like teeth). Extraction error means we have taken out the number from the ledger.

GROSS PAY AND NET PAY

Gross pay is the total wages before any deductions.

Net pay is the total wages after deductions have been made for things like tax, national insurance, and pension payments.

ERROR OF ORIGINAL ENTRY

The error was made from the original invoice or receipt, so was entered into the daybooks incorrectly from the start.

COMPENSATING ERROR

This means that two separate errors were made, but coincidently are for the same amount.

For example, an expense was entered as £10, instead of £110.
And
The bank payment was entered as £20, instead of £120.

Two separate errors, but both equal to £100.

ERROR OF OMISSION

Omission means 'left out'. Error of omission means that the entry was left out completely. No debit and no credit entry.

ERROR OF COMMISSION

The entry was made into the wrong account, but the account was of the correct type.

Motor expense entered as an office expense.

Both are expense accounts, both are debits.

ERROR OF PRINCIPLE

The entry was made into the wrong type of account completely.

A new asset was entered as an office expense.

Both are debits, but one is an asset account, and one is an expense account.

Like error of commission but more serious.

SUBSIDIARY LEDGERS

Also known as MEMORANDUM ACCOUNTS and INDIVIDUAL ACCOUNTS.

These are the 'babies' of the main Receivables Ledger Control Account and Payables Ledger Control Account and each one is a separate account for a customer or supplier.

The total of the subsidiary ledgers should always match the total of the main ledger.

TRANSPOSITION ERROR

The numbers have been transposed or turned around.

456 has been entered as 465.

Sometimes difficult to spot.

INCOME TAX

A tax on an employee's income.

INCOME TAX

A tax on an employee's income.

SUSPENSE ACCOUNT

A temporary account to balance a trial balance usually due to errors.

PART 2

COSTING

FLASHCARDS

FINANCIAL ACCOUNTING

A historic record of the income and expenses of a business; usually compiled every 12 months.

For external use, such as HMRC (tax calculations), potential investors, bank, suppliers, and customers.

MANAGEMENT ACCOUNTING

Information provided for internal use.

Information for management to compare results and make decisions. Any format can be used that suits the business.

COST CENTRE

A department of the business where costs can be attributed, such as the factory or the office.

COST UNIT

A item to which costs can be attributed, such as the wheels for a car, or the legs for a table.

COST CLASSIFICATION BY FUNCTION

Production costs (cost of sales)
Sales and distribution costs
Administrative costs
Finance costs

COST CLASSIFICATION BY ELEMENT

Materials
Labour
Overheads

COST CLASSIFICATION BY NATURE

Direct costs (directly attributable to the unit). Wood to make a table. Indirect costs (not directly attributable to the unit). Receptionist's wages.

COST CLASSIFICATION BY BEHAVIOUR

Fixed costs
Variable costs
Semi-variable costs
Stepped costs (stepped fixed costs)

FIXED COSTS

Not affected by change in activity level. Not affected by how many products the business makes and sells.

Examples would be rent of the building or insurance of the business. These do not change when more units are made.

VARIABLE COSTS

Costs which vary with the level of production.

Example: 2 metres of material to make 1 pair of shorts.
4 metres of material to make 2 pairs of shorts.

SEMI-VARIABLE COSTS

These have a fixed element and a variable element.

Example would be electricity. There is a fixed charge that does not vary with production. There is an amount payable per unit of electricity used.

STEPPED COSTS / STEPPED FIXED COSTS

Fixed to a certain point and then the cost is stepped up.

Example: A warehouse can hold 1,000 finished products, so one warehouse is rented.
If the business needs to store 1,001 units, then a second warehouse needs to be rented, thereby doubling the cost.

HIGH LOW METHOD

The method to separate the semi-variable costs between the fixed and variable elements.
Difference between the highest activity cost and lowest activity cost.
Difference between the highest activity level and the lowest activity level.
Divide the difference between the cost and the units to find the variable cost per unit.
Take the total cost of the highest units, deduct the total variable cost (calculated by the variable cost per unit x the numbers of units).
This will leave the fixed cost.

THE PRODUCTION CYCLE

Raw materials - bought in from suppliers.
Work in progress - raw material being made into products.
Finished goods - items stored in the warehouse or shop ready for sale.

FIFO / LIFO / AVCO

FIFO - First in first out - issues are made from the warehouse to the production department using the oldest stock first.
LIFO - Last in first out - issues are made from the warehouse to the production department using the newest stock first. (not generally tested in exams)
AVCO - Average cost - issues are made from the warehouse to the production department using the average cost of the stock.

OVERTIME PREMIUM

The amount paid over and above the normal hourly rate of the employee.

Example: Normal rate £8. Overtime is paid at time and a half, so £12.

Overtime premium is £4.

OVERTIME PAYMENT

The total amount paid for overtime to an employee.

Example: Normal rate £8. Overtime is paid at time and a half, so £12. Overtime payment is £12.

PIECE RATE

Employees are paid per 'piece'.

Example: Lettuce pickers might be paid 20p for every lettuce picked.

BONUS

An extra amount of money paid to employees when they achieve or exceed a target.

Example: An employee receives a bonus of £1 for every unit they make in excess of the target of 100 units per day.

TIME RATE

Also called 'hourly rate'.

Employees are paid for every hour they work.

Example: A bartender is paid £13 for every hour they work in the bar.

SALARY

Employees are paid a set amount for the whole year.

Example: An accounts assistant is paid £20,000 per year based on an average of 37 hours per week.

COMMISSION

A set amount of percentage given to an employee when they make a sale.

Example: A car salesperson earns £100 every time they sell a car.

BUDGET

A budget is a plan for production, income, expenses, or a combination of all three.

It is used to compare the performance of the plan against the actual results at the end of a fixed period.

VARIANCE

The difference between the budget and the actual income or expenses for a business.

Favourable means positive.

Adverse means negative.

BUFFER INVENTORY

An amount of inventory or stock that is kept in reserve so that the business does not run out of stock completely.

I hope you have found this book useful. If you have any comments or suggestions, please contact me through my Facebook page: Teresa Clarke AAT Tutoring.

You may also like my revision workbooks. These are also available from Amazon in paperback or eBook. Links can be found on my website.
https://www.teresaclarke.co.uk/

Teresa Clarke FMAAT

Printed in Great Britain
by Amazon

49369588R00046